The Sky's Patterns

by Sasha Griffin

Daily Patterns

During the day there is light. At night it is dark. This is a pattern that repeats all the time. The causes of this pattern are the movement of Earth and sunlight.

The Sun and Earth

The Sun is always in the sky. It is there during the day, at night, and in all kinds of weather. The Sun is a **star.** It is a round, glowing ball of hot gases. It gives light and heat to Earth.

Earth is also round like the Sun, but much smaller. It does not make its own light. Earth needs light from the Sun.

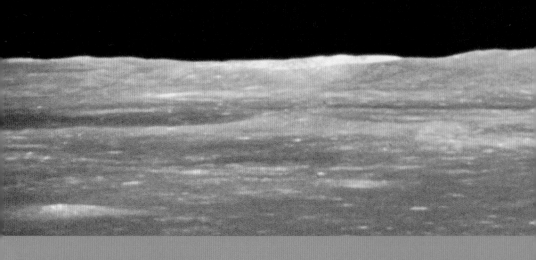

Day and Night

Only half of Earth's round surface faces the Sun at any one time. The part facing the Sun is lit by sunlight. The other half of Earth is dark since it faces away from the Sun.

To us, it looks like the Sun is moving across the sky. However, it is really Earth that is moving.

This photograph of Earth lit by the Sun was taken by Apollo astronauts from the surface of the Moon.

the Sun

Suppose that Earth is a ball of clay, with a pencil running through its center from the top to the bottom. Spin the pencil. Then you can get an idea of how Earth spins around its axis.

Earth's **axis** is an imaginary line that runs through the planet. It passes through the North Pole and the South Pole. Earth spins around its tilted axis. It turns counterclockwise from west to east.

It takes 24 hours for Earth to make one complete **rotation,** or spin around its axis. As it rotates, half of Earth is lit by the Sun. It is daytime for that part of Earth. The half of Earth that is facing away from the Sun is dark. Every part of Earth has day and night during this twenty-four-hour rotation.

Earth always rotates at the same speed. Because of this, the Sun seems to move in predictable patterns across the sky.

The Sun shines on the part of Earth that faces it, giving daylight.

Earth

axis

day

night

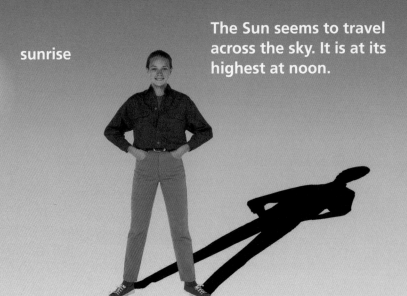

sunrise

The Sun seems to travel across the sky. It is at its highest at noon.

Changing Shadows

As the Sun shines, it creates shadows on Earth. A shadow happens when light, such as sunlight, shines on an object. The object blocks the light. Then a shadow appears on the surface beneath or behind the object. The shadow is the part of the surface that is not getting light.

Shadows are the same shape as the objects that stop the light. Unlike the objects, shadows change length and direction. This is because shadows depend on where the Sun is in the sky.

noon

sunset

Early in the morning the Sun appears in the east. Shadows at this time are long and stretch away from the Sun, toward the west.

Shadows grow shorter as the Sun seems to move higher in the sky. By noon, the Sun appears at its highest. Then shadows are at their shortest. As the Sun keeps moving toward the west, shadows become longer once again. But now they stretch east. This is the opposite direction from the Sun.

Yearly Patterns
Earth's Movement

While Earth spins on its axis, it also revolves around the Sun. One complete trip around the Sun is called a **revolution.** It takes about one year, or 365 days, for Earth to make one revolution.

the four seasons of the year

spring

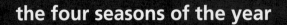

summer

When the northern part of Earth is tilted toward the Sun, it is summer there.

During part of its trip around the Sun, the northern half of Earth tilts toward the Sun. When this happens, the northern half gets the most direct rays of sunlight. It is heated the most. It also has more hours of daylight than darkness each day.

At other times during Earth's trip around the Sun, the southern half of Earth is tilted toward the Sun. Then this part of Earth gets more direct sunlight, heat, and hours of light.

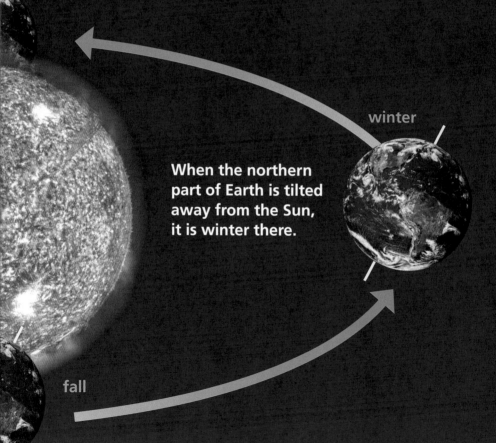

winter

When the northern part of Earth is tilted away from the Sun, it is winter there.

fall

Boston

winter in Boston

Brasília

Making Seasons

Earth's tilted axis and its movement around the Sun cause seasons. Temperatures and amounts of sunlight change in predictable ways throughout the year.

Boston, Massachusetts, tilts toward the Sun in June. This is because it's located on the northern half of Earth. A city on the southern half, such as Brasilia, Brazil, tilts away from the Sun.

Boston is warmer at that time of year because it receives more sunlight. There are more hours of daylight than darkness each day. But in Brasilia it is colder, there is less sunlight, and there are more hours of darkness in a day. We say it is summer in Boston and winter in Brasilia.

As fall grows nearer, Boston receives less sunlight while Brasilia starts to receive more. The amounts of daylight and darkness each day are almost equal in both cities. It is cooler than summer, but warmer than winter.

When Boston points away from the Sun, it is winter. Temperatures are colder, and there are fewer hours of daylight than darkness. When Brasilia points toward the Sun, it is summer. That means more sunlight and warmer temperatures.

The Moon

The Moon is 384,000 kilometers (239,000 miles) away from Earth. That makes it Earth's closest neighbor.

Like Earth, the Moon rotates on its axis. The Moon also revolves around Earth. It takes about 29 days to make one rotation on its axis, and one revolution around Earth.

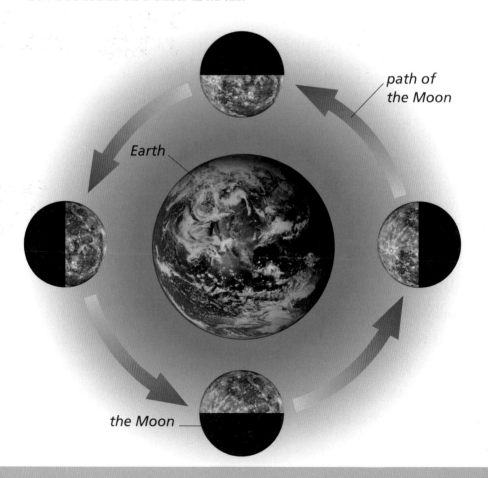

path of the Moon

Earth

the Moon

At night, the Moon is the brightest natural object in the sky. The Moon does not make its own light. It reflects light from the Sun. We can see the Moon because sunlight shines on it and bounces off.

The Moon is always in the sky, and we always see the same side of it. Sometimes we can see it during the day. But it is not as bright as it is at night. This is because the sunlight shining on Earth is brighter than the light that reflects off the Moon.

The Moon's Phases

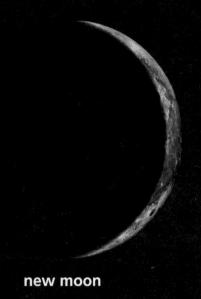

new moon   first quarter

    Sometimes the Moon looks like a bright circle at night. Other times we can't see it at all. The look of the Moon follows a changing pattern. This pattern repeats about every four weeks. Each different way that the Moon looks is called a **phase.**

    Half of the Moon is always lighted by the Sun. But we don't always see the entire lighted half. This is because of the way Earth and the Moon move around each other and the Sun.

full moon　　　　　　　　　**last quarter**

During the phase called the new moon, we cannot see the Moon at all. This is because the Moon is between Earth and the Sun. The dark half of the Moon is facing Earth.

As the Moon continues to revolve, we see a bit more of it each night. About two weeks after the new moon, we are able to see all of the lighted part of the Moon. Now it looks like a circle. This phase is called the full moon. For the next two weeks we see less and less of the Moon until finally it is the new moon again.

A Lunar Eclipse

A **lunar eclipse** happens when Earth moves between the Sun and the Moon. When Earth blocks the Sun's light, it makes a shadow on the Moon. This shadow moves slowly over the Moon's surface until it covers it completely. Then the shadow slowly moves off the Moon. A lunar eclipse is not a phase of the Moon and doesn't happen as often.

When Earth moves between the Sun and the Moon, it blocks the Sun's light.

The Moon will appear reddish in the part of Earth that has nighttime.

The Moon is in Earth's shadow.

the Sun

Earth

the Moon

Star Patterns
Looking at Stars

When you look at the sky on a clear, dark night, you can see thousands of stars. Some of them are larger than the Sun. But they look small because they are trillions of miles away. Some stars are dimmer and harder to see than others. This is because they are the farthest away. It is difficult for our eyes to see them. There are many stars that cannot be seen at all without special tools.

Galileo and the Telescope

A **telescope** is a tool that makes faraway objects appear larger and easier to see. There are different kinds of telescopes. Most try to allow as much light as possible into the telescope. They are made with mirrors that reflect light and lenses that bend light. These telescopes make objects appear bigger and clearer.

Galileo was a scientist who lived in Italy from 1564 to1642. He did not invent the telescope, but he is known for making one that could magnify objects by twenty times. With his telescope, Galileo discovered many new things in space. At that time, most people thought that the Sun revolved around Earth. Galileo's experiments and observations proved that Earth revolves around the Sun.

Galileo made important discoveries about space.

The Hubble Space Telescope floats in space.

The Hubble Space Telescope

While most telescopes are meant to be used on Earth, the Hubble Space Telescope was built for use in space. It is about 600 kilometers (375 miles) above Earth. It revolves around Earth every ninety-seven minutes. Scientists receive pictures and information about space from the Hubble telescope. This has taught them lots about faraway stars and planets in our solar system.

Constellations

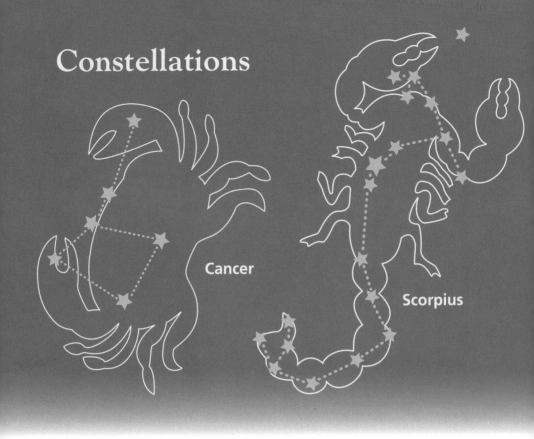

Cancer

Scorpius

Long ago, people noticed that groups of stars made patterns in the sky. These patterns often looked like animals, people, or other things. They gave names to these patterns and made up stories about them. A group of stars that makes a pattern is called a **constellation.** Today we still use many of the constellation names that people created in ancient times. Different groups of people had different names and stories for the constellations. Many of the names and stories came from legends.

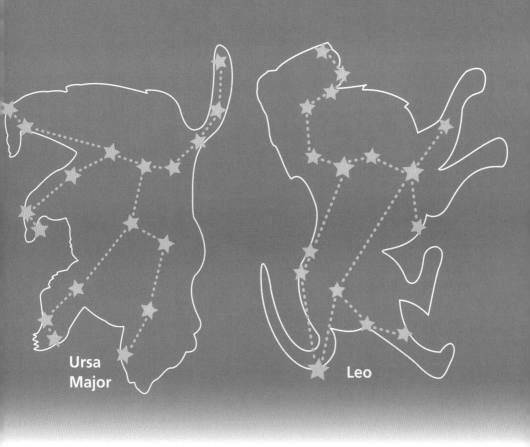

Ursa Major

Leo

One constellation is Ursa Major, which means Great Bear. We can see the Big Dipper in the body and tail of the bear. The story the ancient Greeks told about this constellation was that an angry god turned a woman into a bear. Other cultures told of a girl who turned herself into a bear. Then she chased her sister and brothers. To escape her, they all flew into the sky, where they became the constellation of the Great Bear.

The stars in a constellation may look close together. But they are really very far apart. Because of this, they would not make the same pattern if you looked at them from space.

Earth's movement changes the patterns of stars. As Earth rotates on its axis, the stars appear to move across the sky. The constellations also change position as the seasons change. The constellations in the winter sky are different from those in the summer sky. Only the North Star does not appear to move. This is why people have used the North Star for hundreds of years to help them find their way.

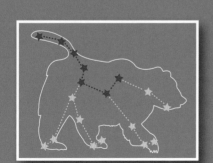

The stars of the Big Dipper help people find the North Star.

spring

summer

fall

winter

The sky has lots of patterns. Earth and the Moon are always following patterns as they move. Earth's movements make it change from day to night and from season to season. We can learn a lot by studying these patterns and other objects in the sky, such as the Sun and stars. Year after year Earth continues to follow some amazing patterns.

Glossary

axis   an imaginary line around which Earth spins.

constellation   a group of stars that make a pattern.

lunar eclipse   when Earth blocks the Sun's light from shining on the Moon.

phase   the different ways the Moon looks.

revolution   the movement of an object, such as Earth, in one complete circle around another object, such as the Sun.

rotation   one complete turn around an axis.

star   a ball of glowing gases that gives off light.

telescope   a tool that magnifies objects that are far away.